The Dominion Design:
The Blueprint for Restoring the Whole Man

-Paul Stone

The Dominion Design © 2025 Paul Stone & Dominion Design LLC. All rights reserved.

No part of this publication may be reproduced, distributed, or transmitted in any form or by any means, including photocopying, recording, or other electronic or mechanical methods, without the prior written permission of the publisher.

Builder's Notice: This manuscript is not a theoretical text; it is a Field Manual. It was excavated by the author, Paul Stone, and refined using the Dominion Design technology stack. It is a living document. As we build the Kingdom, the blueprints evolve. You are holding the Alpha Version. Warning: Do not read this if you are looking for comfort. Read this if you are looking for a shovel.

To the Architect, Who drew the plans before I was born.

To my Wife, Who stayed in the house while I fixed the foundation.

And to my Children, May you never have to excavate this rubble again. This solid ground is my gift to you.

Contents

Note to the Reader: The Foreman's Note — 5

The Blueprint: Accessing the Damage — 6

Part I: The Foundation (The Non-Negotiables)

Chapter 1: The Scholar (Systems of Wisdom) — 13

Chapter 2: The Steward (Systems of Finance) — 22

Chapter 3: The Temple (Systems of Health) — 32

Part II: The Structure (The Instincts)

Chapter 4: The Husband (Instinct of Covenant) — 40

Chapter 5: The Father (Instinct of Discipleship) — 48

Chapter 6: The Entrepreneur (Instinct of Creation) — 56

Part III: The Keystone

Chapter 7: The Man (The System of Systems) — 65

Conclusion: The Groundbreaking — 77

Acknowledgments — 80

Connect with the Brotherhood — 81

The Dominion Keys (Reference Guide) — 82

References — 91

About The Author — 94

Who This Is For

The Foreman's Note: You are not standing in a library; you are standing on a job site. This book is not a lecture; it is a **Work Order**. I am speaking to you as one builder to another. The weight of responsibility in life I am addressing is one I have carried as a husband, a father, and an entrepreneur. However, the systems of Dominion—Wisdom (Scholar), Stewardship (Finance/Time), and Health (Temple)—are universal laws of creation.

If you are a woman reading this to understand the men in your life, or to build your own house, you are welcome here. If you are a single mother acting as both provider and protector, these tools belong to you, too.

The mission of **Dominion** is not just for the man in the mirror, but for the legacy following him. We must equip the next generation with these blueprints now, so they do not have to excavate them later. As wisdom reminds us: *"Train up a child in the way he should go, even when he is old he will not depart from it"* (Proverbs 22:6).

The Blueprint We Build Together

Introduction: The Site Survey

Assessing the Damage

A Personal Note: The Passenger in the Bulldozer

To the man reading this:

I didn't come to this conclusion while sitting in a pew, waiting for a miracle. I came to it because I was drowning. Like many of you, I was successful on paper but chaotic in spirit.

I was efficient at work but exhausted at home. I felt a specific, terrifying sensation that many men feel but never admit:

I felt like a passenger in a bulldozer.

I was moving forward with massive force—crushing deadlines, hitting goals, and driving revenue. I was putting all my effort into a long shot in the dark at being "successful." But when I looked at my personal life, I realized I had no hands on the wheel. I was watching myself crush the peace in my home, flatten my relationships, and burn out my own body, powerless to stop the machine I had built.

The Lost Purpose: Why We Are Restless

Why does this sensation hurt so much? It hurts because it violates your design. Men were created to serve a purpose. We have a burning, innate desire to feel accomplished—to point to a field, a family, or a project and say, "I built that."

The Weight of the Watchman This responsibility is ancient. Men have held a great weight over their heads since the beginning. In the Garden, the man was responsible for guiding Eve to make the right decision. But he failed. He stood by in silence, abdicated his duty, and she ate the fruit.

We are still repeating that silence today. We are the hardworking men who are winning the race but losing the map.

You are caught in the relentless "race to the top." You grind, you achieve, and you provide, but you have never taken the time to fully understand the desires driving you. You are driving a high-performance vehicle at 100 MPH without ever reading the manual.

In the past, men had the environment to cultivate this purpose. They took the time to read the wisdom of scholars. They took the time to explore their faith and comprehend His word.

But most importantly, they had time to excavate their own thoughts in a way that led them closer to the Truth.

The fact is, they listened to real people, not social actors. When they faced the most complicated problems of life, they had large circles of friends—a brotherhood of peers—to help solve them. **Today, that silence is gone. The brotherhood has scattered.**

The cultural noise obscures the truth. Instead of solving problems, we numb them. We spend more time doom-scrolling through the imposter lives of others on social media, medicating our stress, or living in the imposter worlds of video games than we do working on ourselves. We are starving for accomplishment, but we are choking on distraction.

The Diagnostic: The Doctor's Visit

You know how it goes. You go to the doctor for a checkup. He looks at your chart, sees the high blood pressure, the weight gain, the stress markers. But he doesn't want to scare you. So he softens the blow. He says, "You might want to watch your diet," or "Try to get some more rest."

He manages your feelings instead of stating the facts.

I am not that doctor.

The Dominion Design is the lab result that tells you the truth: You are dying because you are eating from the wrong tree. You are consuming the "fruit" of anxiety, hustle, and comparison, and it is poisoning your system. The noise of the world is drowning out the signal of your Creator.

I am not here to soften the blow. I am here to hand you the cure.

The Mission: A Course Correction

I have watched friends, family, parents, and children struggle just trying to figure this out. I have looked at the statistics for men—**suicide, divorce, heart disease, burnout**—and they are terrifying.

I slowly watched myself become a victim of that same cultural and societal noise. I bought the lie that if I just worked harder on the "Idol" (money, status, success), the peace would come. It didn't.

I refuse to continue watching men around the world suffer just trying to figure it out.

It is time we do an about-face course correction. It is time to change our ways, forget about the Idol, and take advantage of the System.

Yes, it should be hard to get there. Nothing worth building is easy. But you choose how hard it is. You can choose the suffering of the Idol (anxiety and collapse) or the discipline of the System (growth and dominion).

The Turning Point: The Hypocrisy of the Architect

I was sitting at my desk late one night, frantically using Artificial Intelligence to build systems for my business. I was designing workflows, safety nets, and protocols to keep the company from crashing.

Suddenly, the hypocrisy hit me like a physical blow.

I was spending 10, 12, 14 hours a day building systems for a business, but I had zero systems for the man running it. I was an Architect at work, but a Passenger at home.

That was the moment everything changed. I didn't open a Bible to "get religious." I opened it to check the data.

I began to cross-reference the most successful, scientifically proven systems for human flourishing with the ancient texts of the Bible. I wanted to see if there was a pattern hiding under the noise. I wanted to see if the "Old Commandment" could survive a modern audit.

The Result: The Myth of the New Miracle

For years, I had been waiting for God to "do something new" in my life. I was waiting for a zap of lightning or a miraculous change in my circumstances.

But looking at the data, I realized the hard truth: **God is not going to "do" anything new. He is already done.**

- In the beginning, He created the System and called it "Good."
- In the end, He sent the Example (Jesus) and said, "It is Finished."

The blueprint is complete. The physics of how life works is set. God isn't working on the system anymore; He is waiting for us to use it.

We are not called to reinvent the wheel. The wheel works perfectly. Our job is to adapt the Ancient Wheel to the Modern Vehicle.

The Excavation: We Are Not Inventing, We Are Remembering

I realized that I didn't need to "become a new man." I needed to excavate the man I was designed to be. Dominion Design is not a self-help book. It is an excavation site.

We are going to dig through the noise to find the Original Factory Settings.

First, we must locate the lost Instruction Manual—the Non-Negotiable Maintenance Pillars required to keep "The Man" operational:

- **The Scholar** (Your Operating System of Truth)
- **The Steward** (Your Management of Resources)
- **The Temple** (Your Physical Hardware)

Then, we will uncover the burning instincts you already feel but don't know how to manage:

- **The Husband** (The Instinct of Covenant)
- **The Father** (The Instinct of Legacy)
- **The Entrepreneur** (The Instinct of Creation)

These are the desires placed in your chest before you were born. But desire without discipline is chaos. We want to equip you to become complete. We want to hand you the tools to build The Man.

This book is the shovel. I am not the Guru. I am not standing on a mountain shouting down at you. I am just a fellow traveler who found a blueprint in the dust, wiped it off, and realized it still works.

I am not asking you to trust me. I am asking you to trust the Data and the Designer. **God finished His work. It's time for you to start yours. Here are the keys.**

— Paul Stone The Dominion Lab

Chapter 1: The Scholar (Systems of Wisdom)

The Sovereign Student: Analyzing the Data of Your Life

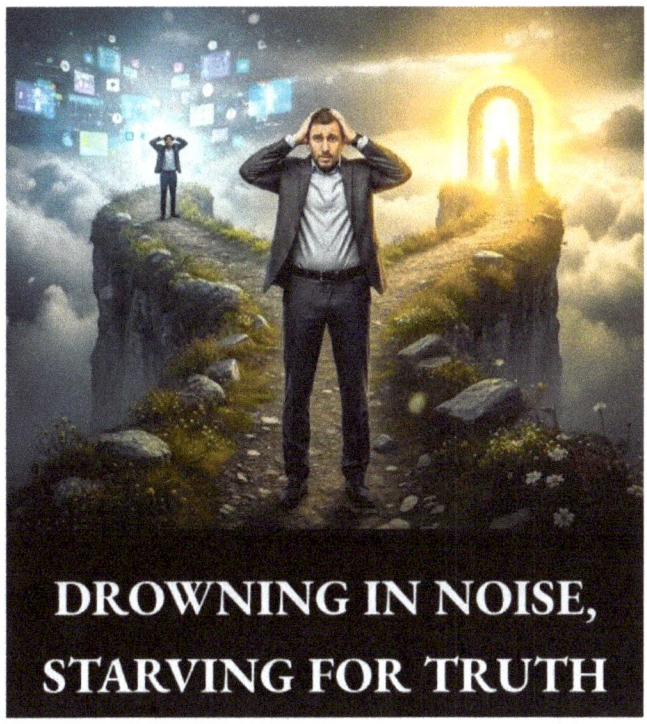

The Immutable Design

"Beloved, I am not writing a new commandment to you, but an old commandment which you have had from the beginning." (1 John 2:7) You are not here to learn a new trick. You are here to remember the truth. The systems of the Scholar are not modern inventions; they are the ancient "Old Commandments" of how reality works. But while the System is old, the Application must be new. You are the one who must take this ancient code and unlock it for the modern world.

The Pain Point: The Facade of Function

We know the look. It is the man who shows up every day—whether he is leading a boardroom, framing a house, or driving a truck through the night. It is the man who is the first to arrive and the last to leave, whether he signs the checks or earns them.

It is the father who smiles at his children while his mind is racing with bills. It is the reliable friend who fixes everyone else's problems but has no one to call for his own.

To the world, he is a fortress. He is the rock everyone leans on. **But inside? He is breaking down.**

You are drowning in noise but starving for truth. You have access to every answer in human history via the device in your pocket, yet you feel paralyzed. You are caught in a loop of "**Analysis Paralysis,**" terrified that one wrong decision will topple the fragile life you've built.

Research confirms that while we assume more thinking leads to better results, overthinking effectively breaks the flow of interaction and prevents prompt action (Talbert, 2017).

You are smart, capable, and hardworking—so why does your mind feel like a chaotic browser with a thousand tabs open?

The Crisis: Garbage In, Garbage Out

I know this friction. As a man who has built businesses and navigated the complexities of a family, I spent years trying to outthink my problems. I thought life was an equation: collect enough facts, and the solution would reveal itself.

But I was wrong. There is a universal rule that applies to everything—from engine repair to accounting: **Garbage In, Garbage Out** (Lidwell et al., 2010). If the fuel is bad, the engine won't run. If the ingredients are rotten, the meal is spoiled.

Most men are operating on corrupted ingredients. We consume fear-based news, comparison-based social media, and advice from people who haven't built anything worth emulating. We lack a **filtration system**.

In my own experience, I learned the danger of "imposter participants"—people or sources that sneak into your decision-making process and give fake answers. If you don't catch them, they ruin the entire project. Studies on **"self-persuasion"** show that we are easily influenced by irrelevant experts if we do not have a strong internal standard (Schwardmann et al., 2022).

Life is exactly the same. We have "imposters" all around us:

- The **toxic friend**, giving relationship advice while his own marriage is failing.
- The **financial "guru"** promising quick riches while you go broke.
- The **inner voice** telling you that you aren't good enough.

The Aha Moment: The Contaminated Supply Chain

You do not have a resource problem; you have a **filtration problem**. You are trying to build a life of Dominion using bad data—counterfeit materials from a world that sells you outrage and envy instead of truth. But here is the good news: **You don't need to waste time analyzing the poison.** You don't need to figure out why the supply chain is corrupted or spend years dissecting the noise. **Enough thinking.** The solution is not to analyze the trash; the solution is to close the gate. You simply need a filter that rejects the counterfeit material before it ever enters your mind.

The Universal Instinct: The Filter

The Scholar is not just about reading books. It is the Instinct of Filtration. You use this instinct every day: when you vet a business deal, when you judge a friend's character, or when you decide what food to put in your mouth. It is the Guardian of the Gate.

The Architect's Tool: The Compass

Think of your mind like a digital compass. It works by detecting "True North." But if you wake up and immediately hold a giant magnet (your phone, the news, social media) next to the compass, the needle goes crazy. By noon, your "True North" is off by 20 degrees, and you are walking in circles.

The psychological concept of **Anchor Bias** proves that our brains latch onto the first piece of information we hear (The Decision Lab, 2024). If your anchor is the magnet, you drift. The Scholar Protocol isn't about being smarter; it's about removing the magnet so you can see where you're actually going.

The Solution: The Fear of the Lord Protocol

If we are to filter the noise effectively, we need a "North Star"—a standard of truth that never changes. In my own search for truth, I found that Allowing God's word to guide you transforms your perception toward the truth, which will guide you to make better decisions.

Biblical Truth*: "The fear of the Lord is the beginning of wisdom" (Proverbs 9:10).*

This is not being scared of God; it's respecting His "data" above all else. It's acknowledging that the Creator knows more about how life works than the culture does. Furthermore, in Christ "*are hidden all the treasures of wisdom and knowledge*" *(Colossians 2:3).*

The Prerequisite: The Life-Long Audit

The Scholar Pillar is not a class you pass; it is a protocol you live. My childhood environment taught me to verify everything. I realized that wisdom isn't a destination where you suddenly "know it all." True wisdom is the humble admission that you don't know, followed by the disciplined pursuit of the Source who does.

You must view yourself as a **Sovereign Student**. This realization is the prerequisite for everything else. You cannot be a stable **Steward** (Finance) or a faithful **Husband** (Covenant) until you learn how to separate the truth from the lies. As the man on the front line, you must consistently practice righteous judgment to identify the outliers and maintain integrity.

The Site Inspection: The Structural Audit

In construction, you never complete a project without a third-party inspection. You might think your math is perfect, but if you are wrong, the building collapses. A Brother acts as your Independent Inspector. He isn't criticizing your blueprints to be mean; he is stress-testing your logic to make sure the roof doesn't cave in on your family. You cannot build this life alone. You need an audit before you break ground.

The Protocol: The 15-Minute Truth Audit

You cannot fix your whole life today, but you can fix your input stream. We must move from passive consumption to active choices.

- **The Trigger:** Immediately upon waking, before your feet hit the floor.
- **The Restriction:** Do not look at your phone, email, news, or social media. This prevents the world from setting your "Anchor" for the day.
- **The Action:** Dedicate the first 15 minutes solely to a Primary Source Text **(Scripture).**

This is the first step in "renewing your mind" (Romans 12:2, NASB).

INTERACTIVE AUDIT: THE ARCHITECT'S LOG

Use the space below to conduct your first audit.

1. **The Input Analysis:** What was the first thing you looked at this morning?

   _____

   How did that information make you feel? (Anxious, Angry, Envious, Numb?)

   _____

2. **The Source Check:** Who is the "Imposter Participant" currently influencing your decisions? (A news anchor, a toxic friend, a social media account?)

   _____

3. **The Commitment:** "For the next 7 days, I commit to giving the first 15 minutes of my day to the Truth, not the Noise." Signed:

   _____

Why This Works

This works because the Scholar is the upstream valve for your entire life. If the water is poisoned at the source, it doesn't matter how expensive the plumbing is in the house (The Steward) or how hard you work in the garden (The Entrepreneur)—everything downstream dies.

By securing the Scholar, you are not just learning facts; you are protecting the integrity of every other pillar. You are ensuring that when you teach your son how to handle money, or your daughter how to choose a husband, you are pulling from a reservoir of eternal Truth, not the polluted stream of current culture. **You cannot transmit what you do not possess**. This protocol ensures that the map you hand to the next generation is accurate, tested, and true.

The Next Step

Now that your mind is clear, you will start to see the cracks in your foundation. The greatest source of anxiety for most men isn't what they know, but what they owe. It is time to secure your resources.

Let's move to Pillar 2: The Steward.

Chapter 2: The Steward (Systems of Finance)

The Sovereign Manager:

Aligning Your Resources with Your Revelation

The Pain Point: The Scarcity Loop

You have followed the protocol of the Sovereign Student (Chapter 1). The mental noise has started to clear, and you are beginning to filter truth from lies. But clarity is only half the battle. Now that your mind is becoming ordered, you are likely feeling the acute friction of your material reality.

You are smart, you are capable, and you may even be outwardly successful. Yet, you wake up every morning with a low-grade, constant dread regarding your resources. This is not just about the numbers in your bank account; it is a pervasive anxiety about **capacity.**

- **The Zero-Sum Trap:** You feel like you are perpetually running a game where every gain in one area (e.g., career profit) results in an equal loss somewhere else (e.g., family time or health).
- **The Tunnel Vision:** You are haunted by the **"Scarcity Mindset,"** a psychological phenomenon where the obsession with a lack of resources actually reduces your cognitive bandwidth, making you less capable of solving the problem (Mullainathan & Shafir, 2013).
- **The Output Trap:** You measure your worth by your output, convinced that if you just acquire more, the fear will finally go away.

This is the trap. You are trying to solve a spiritual and systemic problem with a mathematical solution. You think you need more money, more hours, or more talent. But the data suggests otherwise.

The Crisis: The Hedonic Treadmill

Why do we fall into this trap? Why does the "next big check" or the "promotion" never actually satisfy the anxiety?

Psychologists call this the **Hedonic Treadmill.** Humans have a tendency to quickly return to a relatively stable level of happiness despite major positive or negative events or life changes (Brickman & Campbell, 1971). You get the raise, and for three months, you feel safe. But soon, your lifestyle expands to consume the new resource, the novelty wears off, and the anxiety returns.

The Inherited Script: I learned this the hard way. My childhood was defined by a chaotic relationship with resources. I watched my parents struggle—not because they were bad people, but because they lacked a design. As a boy, I looked at other families who had "more"—better cars, bigger houses—and my unaware, developing mind created a false equation:

Value = Possessions.

I believed the peace I saw in others was a result of the items they owned. This is the crisis many men face: we are operating on an inherited script that says peace is found in the accumulation of things, rather than the management of resources.

But this isn't just a ghost from the past. We are reminded of this script every single day by the societal noise. If you do not apply the **Scholar's Filter** (Chapter 1) to your inputs, the world will convince you that you are one purchase away from happiness. The commercials, the social media feeds, and the cultural signals are all designed to reinforce the lie that "More Stuff = More Peace." Without the Filter, you are fighting a losing battle against a billion-dollar marketing machine.

The Breakdown: System Failure

We attempt to "out-earn" our chaos. We seek financial freedom by chasing market trends and quick schemes, viewing money, time, and talent as separate entities to be captured rather than integrated resources to be managed.

This approach is doomed because it violates the **Law of Entropy** (Second Law of Thermodynamics). In physics, this law states that isolated systems naturally evolve toward thermal equilibrium—meaning they decline into disorder and chaos unless energy is actively applied to maintain them (Çengel & Boles, 2015). Your finances, your schedule, and your energy are no different. Without a governance system, they will naturally decay into chaos.

The Bankruptcy of the Soul: I carried my childhood script into adulthood. I tried to fill the void with acquisition. I worked harder, bought more, and chased external markers of success. But because I lacked a system of governance, I drove my life off a cliff. I repeated my parents' cycle perfectly, landing in bankruptcy.

I had hit rock bottom. I had no money, but worse, I had no peace.

But let me be clear: You do not have to file Chapter 11 to be bankrupt. You may have a full bank account but a bankrupt soul. You may have perfect credit but zero peace. Whether you are literally broke or emotionally spent, the cause is the same: System Failure.

It was in that pit that I realized the fatal flaw in my thinking: I had been obsessed with the items (the output), but I had completely ignored the governance (the system). A man's dominion is not measured by what he holds in his hand, but by how he manages what is in his care.

The Aha Moment: The Family Trust

The true liberation in the Steward Pillar comes from a shift in identity. You must move from the anxiety of the **Owner** to the authority of the **Trustee**.

In the business world, a **Fiduciary** is a person or organization that acts on behalf of another person, putting their clients' interests ahead of their own (Legal Information Institute, 2023). A Fiduciary does not panic when the market shifts because the assets are not theirs; their only job is to manage them according to the Owner's instructions.

But we must take this deeper. You are not just a manager; you are the Trustee of a Legacy.

1. **The Grantor (God):** He owns the resource eternally. He sets the rules.
2. **The Trustee (You):** You hold the resource temporarily. Your job is to grow it and protect it.
3. **The Beneficiaries (Your Lineage):** These are the Future Owners.

The Architect's Perspective: The Orchard

A day-trader thinks about lunch; a farmer thinks about the next decade. If you plant an apple tree today, you won't eat the fruit—your kids will. True Stewardship is planting financial trees that you may never sit under. You aren't building wealth to buy toys; you are building a "Family Trust"—a resource system that ensures your grandchildren start the race ten steps ahead of where you started. When you waste money, you aren't just spending your paycheck; you are eating the seed corn of your children's harvest.

Biblical Truth: The Parable of the Talents

"For it is just like a man about to go on a journey, who called his own servants and entrusted his possessions to them... Now after a long time the master of those servants came and settled accounts with them" (Matthew 25:14, 19, NASB).

The Master (God) owns the resource. You (The Steward) manage it. The "fearful servant" was the one who hid the resource because he misunderstood the Master's character. The "good and faithful servant" was the one who actively managed and multiplied it.

The Revelation: You are not the Owner. You are the Fund Manager for God's estate. When you accept this, the pressure to "prove yourself" vanishes. Your worth is no longer tied to your net worth, but to your faithfulness. "It is required of stewards that one be found trustworthy" (1 Corinthians 4:2, NASB).

The Solution: The 80/10/10 Protocol

To break the Scarcity Loop and step into Fiduciary Dominion, we need a "Universal Operating System" for resources. This applies to your money, your schedule, and your energy. This system creates artificial boundaries that force you to prioritize.

The Site Constraint: The MacGyver Protocol You might fear that living on 80% restricts your freedom. However, psychology teaches us the concept of **Constraint-Driven Innovation** (Stokes, 2005). When we have infinite options or resources, we often suffer from decision paralysis or waste. However, when we face a hard constraint (like a limited budget or deadline), the brain is forced to think creatively to solve the problem.

Give a man a million dollars and infinite time, and he will waste half of it on bad ideas. Give a man a paperclip, a stick of gum, and 30 seconds to defuse a bomb, and he becomes a genius. This is the **MacGyver Effect**. By artificially constraining your resources to 80%, you force your mind to become efficient. You stop solving problems by "throwing money at them" and start solving them with wisdom.

The Ultimate Constraint: The System of Sabbath

There is one final constraint that separates the Steward from the Slave: **The Sabbath.**

The world says, "Hustle 24/7." God's system says, "Work six, rest one."

This is not just religious tradition; it is a **Constraint System**. The principle is primarily explained by **Parkinson's Law,** which states that "work expands to fill the time available for its completion" (Parkinson, 1955).

If you give yourself seven days to do a job, it will take seven days. If you force yourself to do it in six, you become lean, focused, and efficient. Stopping your work is the ultimate act of trust in the Hero. It declares that the universe is held together by His word, not your email responsiveness. It reminds you that **He is the Provider; you are just the Manager.**

INTERACTIVE AUDIT: THE ARCHITECT'S LEDGER

The Premise: You are managing two accounts. One is renewable (Money); one is depleting (Time). Most men audit their bank statements down to the penny but have no idea where their hours are bleeding out. **You cannot manage what you do not measure.**

The Trigger: Open your financial and time tracking data immediately following your Truth Audit.

The Questions:

1. The Capital Ledger (Financial Assets): Look at your last 30 days. Is it an 80/10/10 split? [ ] Yes [ ] No Identify the Leak: What is one recurring "Weed Expense" (subscription, habit, luxury) you can cut today to fund the Future?

2. The Chronos Ledger (Time Assets): Look at your "Investment" hours vs. your "Entropy" (Waste) hours. Are you scrolling more than you are building? [ ] Yes [ ] No The Sabbath Check: When was the last time you went 24 hours without checking the "Operations" bucket?

The Double-Lock Commitment: "I refuse to eat the seed. I commit to living on 80% and treating my Time as my most expensive currency."

Signed:

_____

Why This Works

This works because it aligns your internal psychology with your external reality. **You are finite; God is infinite.** When you try to play the role of the Infinite Owner—carrying the weight of every outcome—you burn out. Your mind fragments (Scholar) and your body breaks (Temple) because you are carrying a load you were not designed to bear.

By accepting the role of the Steward, you transfer the weight of the Outcome to the Owner, while you focus purely on the Process. This does not just fix your bank account; it fixes your sleep. It moves you from the crushing anxiety of "Survival of the Fittest" to the peaceful diligence of "Faithfulness to the Master." You stop worshipping the creation and start serving the Creator.

The Next Step

Once you have established the clarity of The Scholar and the operational integrity of The Steward, you are ready to address the fundamental machine that runs both systems: your body and mind. You cannot steward a fortune if the vessel holding it is broken.

It is time to move to Pillar 3: The Temple.

Chapter 3: The Temple (Systems of Health)

The Structural Machine: Governing the Vessel of Dominion

The Pain Point: The Cracking Foundation

You have begun the process of filtration as a Sovereign Student (Chapter 1) and have started to govern your resources as a Fiduciary Steward (Chapter 2). But as you attempt to scale your dominion, you encounter a silent, internal resistance. You have the blueprint and the resources, but the "machine" required to execute the work is failing.

- **The Ghost in the Machine:** You are mentally sharp, yet you feel like a "ghost in a decaying machine"—your mind wants to build, but your body lacks the energy to follow through.
- **Decision Fatigue:** You suffer from cognitive decline because your physiological "hardware" is depleted of the essential resources—sleep, nutrition, and movement—required for high-level processing.
- **The Vanity Trap:** You view your health as an optional luxury (vanity) rather than the primary structural infrastructure (utility) that supports every other pillar of your life.

This is the Crisis of the Broken Vessel. Many men attempt to build empires while their physical foundation is crumbling. They treat their bodies like a rented car they intend to return trashed, rather than the sacred machine designed for high-performance dominion.

The Structural Insight: The Load-Bearing Beam

In any house, there is a beam that carries the weight of the floors above it. It isn't pretty; it's buried in the basement. But if that beam cracks, the roof (your business), the second floor (your family), and the walls (your legacy) all come down.

Your body is that beam. Training isn't about looking good in a t-shirt; it's about **Structural Integrity**. In engineering, "structural health monitoring" is required to prevent catastrophic failure under load (Huston, 2010). You train so that when the weight of life lands on your shoulders, you don't snap and bring the whole house down on your wife and kids.

The Crisis: The Maintenance Debt

The Drift: In my youth, my relationship with my "Temple" was simple: I ate, played, and slept. My body was a self-maintaining engine I took for granted. But as the weight of adulthood increased, "play" became "rest" (sedentary consumption), and "fuel" became "comfort" (emotional eating).

The Denial: When I sought medical help for chronic headaches and brain fog, the doctor's answer was standard: eat better, sleep more, exercise. I ignored him. I looked at "high-performers" and saw men grinding on four hours of sleep and caffeine. I believed the lie that to be a man of impact, I had to sacrifice the vessel for the mission.

The Breakdown: The system eventually forced a shutdown. Weight gain, heart palpitations, and high cholesterol were the warning lights I could no longer ignore. I realized that the answers were not hidden; they were foundational truths repeated in Scripture and echoed by the brightest scientific minds. I was trying to run a million-dollar life on a ten-cent battery.

The Aha Moment: Hardware-Software Integration

The breakthrough in the Temple Pillar is understanding that your body is not a "distraction" from your spiritual or intellectual work—it is the hardware that runs it. If the Scholar (Chapter 1) is your "software" (wisdom and data), the Temple is the "processor." **You cannot run advanced software on corrupted hardware.**

The Biological Bridge to Wisdom: There is a direct correlation between your physical state and your ability to remain a Sovereign Student. When you exercise, your body produces a protein called **Brain-Derived Neurotrophic Factor (BDNF)**. Scientists refer to BDNF as "Miracle-Gro for the brain" because it is essential for neuroplasticity—the brain's ability to learn, remember, and grow (Erickson et al., 2011). Furthermore, exercise has been proven as a primary treatment for anxiety, clearing the mental fog that clouds judgment (Rebar et al., 2015)

The Mechanical Insight: The Cold Engine

Have you ever tried to start a diesel truck in freezing temperatures without letting the glow plugs warm up? It sputters and dies. Your brain is that engine. If you sit at a desk all day (cold), your cognitive engine stalls.

Exercise is the glow plug. It warms the system, releases BDNF, and prepares the "processor" to handle the heavy load of the Scholar's work. You don't move just to burn calories; you move to start the engine.

Without the physical movement of the Temple, the "Scholar" becomes stagnant. Your ability to continue learning and "renewing your mind" is biologically throttled by physical neglect. Taking care of the "system" is the only way to keep the mind open to the revelation required for dominion.

The Fiduciary Body Just as we shifted from "Owner" to "Fiduciary" in our finances, we must do the same with our physical forms. Your body is not your own to destroy. **It is the only vehicle capable of transporting your legacy to the next generation.**

If you run this machine into the ground today, you are robbing your children of the leader they need tomorrow. A Fiduciary preserves the asset because he knows the beneficiaries—your lineage—are relying on the decisions he makes right now. Every time you choose maintenance over negligence, you are ensuring that the wisdom of the Scholar and the wealth of the Steward actually reach their destination.

You must maintain structural integrity not just to survive the day, but to ensure you are standing tall when it is time to hand off the baton.

Biblical Truth: "Or do you not know that your body is a temple of the Holy Spirit who is in you, whom you have from God, and that you are not your own? For you have been bought with a price: therefore glorify God in your body" (1 Corinthians 6:19-20, NASB).

The Solution: The 168 Maintenance Protocol To ensure the structural integrity of your Temple, we manage the 168 hours of the week with the same precision we manage the 80/10/10 financial protocol.

The Three Pillars of the Temple System:

1. **Systemic Recovery (The 56-Hour Rule):** Sleep is not "wasted time"; it is a systemic reset. Sleep deprivation impairs the prefrontal cortex—the "Scholar's" seat of logic and impulse control (Walker, 2017). A Dominion Engineer prioritizes 7–8 hours of recovery to clear "biological garbage" from the hardware.
2. **Fuel Quality (The Clean Ingredient Protocol):** Recalling GIGO (Garbage In, Garbage Out), the Temple requires high-grade fuel. We move away from "comfort" consumption and treat nutrition as a chemical input for high-level output.
3. **Structural Loading (The Resistance Protocol):** The human body requires "controlled stress" to maintain integrity. Systematic resistance training is the "maintenance work" that ensures the machine can carry the load of leadership for decades, not just years.

The Brotherhood Hint: The Spotter Here is the first rule of heavy structural work: **Never lift alone**. In the gym, you can only push to your absolute limit if you have a Spotter—someone watching the bar to make sure it doesn't crush your throat. This is a law of physics that applies to life. We often fail in our health because we are trying to lift the weight in isolation. To build a Temple that lasts, you will eventually need a Brother to spot you. (We will build this crew together in The Dominion Lab).

INTERACTIVE AUDIT: THE MACHINE LOG

The Premise: Stop viewing your body through the lens of Vanity (how I look). View it through the lens of Integrity (how I function).

The Trigger: During your morning 15-Minute Truth Audit, perform this quick systems check.

The Questions:

1. **Recovery Check:** Did the machine get 7+ hours of shutdown time

last night? [ ] Yes [ ] No If No, what "Entropy Activity" (TV, Phone) stole the time?

2. **Fuel Check:** Identify two "comfort foods" that act as corrupted fuel in your current diet.

3. **The Linkage Experiment:** For the next 3 days, perform 30 minutes of movement and immediately follow it with 15 minutes of Scholar study. Record the difference in mental clarity below.

The Maintenance Oath: "I recognize this vessel is not my own. I commit to maintaining the machine so it can carry the weight of my calling."

Signed:
_____

Why This Works

This works because it removes **Ego** from the equation. When health is about "looking good," it is easy to quit when you get busy or discouraged. But when health is about **Structural Integrity**—ensuring the house doesn't fall on your family—it becomes non-negotiable. You are not training for a beach body; you are training to be a durable instrument in the hands of God.

The Next Step

The Scholar is clear. The Steward is organized. The Temple is reinforced. You are finally equipped to handle the heaviest load a man can carry: the heart of another human being.

It is time to move to **Pillar 4: The Husband (Systems of Covenant).**

Chapter 4: The Husband (Instinct of Covenant)

The Lead Partner: Architecting Dominion in Relationships

The Pain Point: The Transactional Trap

You have optimized your mind (The Scholar), organized your resources (The Steward), and strengthened your vessel (The Temple). But now you step into the sphere of **High-Stakes Relationships.** Whether this is a marriage, a serious courtship, or a critical business partnership, you are encountering a friction that systems of logic alone cannot solve.

- **The Passenger Syndrome:** You are "successful" by every external metric, yet you feel like a passenger in your own home.
- **The Contract Fallacy:** You treat your covenants like transactional exchanges: 'I provided the capital (or the paycheck) and did my job, so why am I not receiving the dividend of loyalty and peace?' You fail to realize that humans are not vending machines.
- **The Emotional Bankruptcy**: You are physically present but emotionally bankrupt, defaulting to a "transactional" model where you only give as much as you believe you are receiving.

The Crisis: The Argument Legacy

The Inherited Script I grew up watching a blueprint of dysfunction. My parents' relationship was defined by a constant tug-of-war over opinions. These weren't just disagreements; they were battles for "The Truth." Because neither side could step outside their own ego to see the other's perspective, logic was abandoned. The friction eventually became too great for the structure to hold, and it led to separation.

The Repetition: Like a corrupted file being copied to a new hard drive, I carried this script into my early relationships and the first years of my marriage. Every conflict became a trial where I was the prosecutor, the judge, and the jury. I was obsessed with being "right." I believed that "standing firm" was a sign of strength, when in reality, it was a sign of structural rigidity. My "Lead Partner" role was failing because I was trying to rule a domain rather than architect a covenant.

The Systemic Shift: The Humility Protocol

The "Aha Moment" came when I realized that my need to be "right" was actually a lack of Dominion Design. I discovered a new system rooted in **Humility.**

I stopped entering conversations to win and started entering them to understand. I realized that the strongest man in the room is not the one who shouts his opinion the loudest, but the one who has the capacity to fully hold another person's perspective before asserting his own.

The Integration: Relying on the Maintenance Pillars

This shift to a "Humility System" is not a personality trait; it is a systemic output of your first three pillars. Without them, your ego will always revert to the "Right vs. Wrong" script.

1. **The Scholar Link (Intellectual Humility):** In Chapter 1, we learned to filter "Noise" from "Truth." In a relationship, your own ego is often the "Noise." Intellectual humility—the recognition that your perspective is limited—is a Scholar's discipline. It allows you to treat your partner's perspective as vital data rather than a threat to your authority.

2. **The Steward Link (Emotional Resource Management):** **You** have 168 hours a week (The Temple). If you waste 10 of those hours in circular arguments because you refuse to listen, you are a poor Steward. Humility is a "Time-Saving System." By understanding first, you bypass the hours of friction that lead to "Systemic Separation."

3. **The Temple Link (Physiological Regulation):** You cannot practice humility if your body is in a "Fight or Flight" state. When you are depleted, your brain's amygdala takes over, making empathy biologically impossible. A strong Temple (Chapter 3) allows you to stay calm, lowering your heart rate so the "Scholar" can engage.

The Structural Insight: The Relief Valve

Industrial boilers have a relief valve. When the pressure gets too high, the valve opens to let off steam so the machine doesn't explode.

In a marriage or a strategic alliance, pressure builds. If you don't have a brother to talk to—a safe place to vent your frustration and get a reality check—you will explode within your own camp. Whether you are leading a family or a company, you cannot carry the weight of a covenant alone. You need a crew to check your pressure gauges.

The Aha Moment: The Power of the Second Chair

The breakthrough in the Husband Pillar is realizing that Humility is a System of Governance. To lead, you must first serve.

Scholarly Evidence: Psychological research into **Cognitive Empathy**—the ability to identify and understand another's mental state—shows that it is the primary driver of conflict resolution. A study on the "Speaker-Listener Technique" proved that when a partner feels "accurately mirrored," their defensiveness drops significantly, allowing for logical, collaborative decision-making (Markman et al., 2010).

Biblical Truth: This is the "Dominion of Humility" described in Scripture. It is not about being a doormat; it is about having the strength to prioritize the Entity over the Ego. "Do nothing from selfishness or empty conceit, but with humility of mind regard one another as more important than yourselves". (Philippians 2:3-4, NASB).

The Solution: The Covenant Operating System (C.O.S.)

(Note: While this protocol is designed for the home, it is the exact same mechanism used to save failing business partnerships and deepen serious friendships.)

To move from "The Argument Legacy" to "The Covenant Leader," we implement the **C.O.S.** protocol.

1. **The Perspective Mirror (The Scholar/Humility System)** Before you are allowed to state your "Right" opinion in a conflict, you must first state your partner's perspective back to them until they say, "Yes, that is exactly how I feel." This system forces the "Scholar" to process data before the "Ego" reacts.

2. **The 5:1 Positive Ratio (Stewardship of Connection)** As discussed, you must manage your "Emotional Bank Account." For every one withdrawal (a critique or disagreement), you must have five deposits (affirmations). If you are "Overdrawn," the structure will crack (Gottman, 1994).

3. **The Weekly Domain Sync (Governance)** Every Sunday, you sit as the "Lead Partner" to align the week. You are not there to give orders; you are there to ensure the "Entity" is healthy. You audit the Calendar, the Budget, and the Heart.

The Technician's Insight: The Bomb Squad

When the Bomb Squad shows up, they don't yell, "I'm right!" They ask, "Is it the red wire or the blue wire?" They are hunting for Data, not Dominance.

An argument with your wife is a bomb. If you try to dominate it, it blows up in your face. If you use the Perspective Mirror to get the data, you defuse it. Be the Technician, not the Dictator.

INTERACTIVE AUDIT: THE COVENANT LOG

The Premise: In any high-stakes relationship (Marriage, Business, or Courtship), you are forbidden from saying "I'm right" or "You're wrong." You are only allowed to seek Data.

The Trigger: During your next conflict or negotiation.

The Questions:

1. The Mirror Test: Stop talking. Listen to your counterpart for 5 minutes. Then say, "What I hear you saying is [Mirror their thoughts]. Did I get that right?" Do not move forward until they say yes. [ ] I completed the Mirror Test.

2. The Scholar Check: Ask yourself: "Is my stance based on Truth (Chapter 1) or am I just trying to win the argument?"

3. The Temple Check: Is your chest tightening? If yes, take 10 minutes of silence to regulate your hardware before re-engaging. [ ] Regulated [ ] Failed

The Covenant Oath: "I commit to being the Lead Partner. I will prioritize the health of the Covenant over the victory of my Ego."

Signed:

_____

Why This Works

This works because it breaks the "Adversarial Loop." Most high-stakes relationships fail—whether in the home or the office—because the partners view each other as opponents in a courtroom.

By using the **Perspective Mirror**, you shift the dynamic from "Me vs. You" to "Us vs. The Problem." You become Allies. When a human being feels heard, they feel safe. And whether it is a wife, a fiancée, or a strategic partner, **safety is the prerequisite for loyalty**. You cannot lead someone who is busy defending themselves against you.

The Next Step

When the Lead Partner masters the System of Humility, the home stops being a battlefield and starts being a base of operations. Now, we expand that dominion to the next generation.

It is time to move to Pillar 5: The Father (Instinct of Legacy).

Chapter 5: The Father (Instinct of Discipleship)

The Master Builder: From Trial and Error to Architectural Intent

The Pain Point: The Legacy of the "Friendly" Ghost

Most men approach the role of the Patriarch—whether as a father, a manager, or a mentor—like an apprentice who was never given a manual. You are building a skyscraper based on a "feeling," hoping it doesn't fall down..

- **The Ghost (The Void):** You may have grown up with a biological father or a professional mentor who was non-existent—a literal void where a foundation should have been. You learned to survive, but you never learned to build.

- **The Friend(The Enabler):** You may have had a stepfather or a "cool boss" who functioned more as a peer than a pillar. He provided kindness (he bought the pizza or the beer) but he lacked the Systems of Discipline and the Manual of Guidance required to forge high-performance character. He wanted to be liked more than he understood the assignment.

- **The Trial and Error(The Gambler):** You are raising your children (or leading your team) through "the madness," figuring it out as you go. Your people are surviving, but you realize their success is a testament to luck or grace rather than design. You are realizing that a simpler, more powerful system was available all along.

This is the Crisis of the Accidental Legacy. Whether you are raising a son or raising a successor in your company, the error is the same: We treat leadership as an emotional reaction rather than a **Discipleship System**. The instructions haven't been missing; they have been waiting to be integrated into your Dominion Design.

The Crisis: The Manual in Plain Sight

The Personal Script My early years of parenting were defined by "Trial and Error." Because I lacked a clear model of a father who provided both Presence and Protocol, I had to learn the hard way. I eventually discovered that the "madness" of parenting isn't a mystery to be solved—it's a system to be implemented.

The instructions for building a human are found in the same place we found the instructions for the mind: in the Truth. When I shifted from "winging it" to following the "Architect's Manual," the stress of parenting was replaced by the clarity of discipleship.

The Integration: Relying on the Maintenance Pillars A Father is simply a Scholar, Steward, and Temple whose "User Base" has expanded. If you cannot lead yourself, you cannot disciple a child.

1. **The Scholar Link (The System Teacher):** The Father's primary job is to teach the child how to think, not what to think. You are the "Lead Scholar" of the home. You take the "Truth Filtering" system from Chapter 1 and install it into your children.
2. **The Steward Link (The Character Investor):** A Steward manages assets. Your children are "Legacy Assets." If you are a high-level manager at work but a poor manager of your child's character, you are "Embezzling" the time that belongs to their future.
3. **The Temple Link (The Calm Hardware):** Children are experts at testing hardware. If your "Temple" is weak, your

fuse is short. Your physical and emotional discipline is the "Shock Absorber" that allows the home to remain stable during their "Trial and Error" phases.

The Foreman's Perspective: The Site Consultant

Even the best CEO has a Board of Directors. Why? Because sometimes the team (your kids) gets tired of hearing the CEO's voice.

Your son needs an **"External Consultant"**—an uncle, a mentor, or a trusted friend who reinforces your values but speaks with a different voice. He isn't replacing you; he is validating you. Don't let your pride prevent you from bringing in outside experts to help build your legacy.

The Universal Application: Leading by Example

The Father Pillar is the blueprint for all leadership. Whether you are a dad, a manager, or a CEO, the system is the same: **Discipleship through Modeling**.

In the corporate world, a manager who acts as a "friend" without discipline (The Stepdad Model) creates a chaotic, low-performance team. A manager who is "non-existent" (The Ghost Model) creates a fearful, unguided team. The Dominion Father model—**High Standards combined with High Support**—is the gold standard for management. You cannot "manage" people if you cannot "father" (disciple) them into their best selves.

The Evidence: The Power of Presence and Protocol

Scholarly Evidence:

- **Social Learning Theory:** Albert Bandura (1977) demonstrated that children learn primarily through observation and modeling. If you tell your child to be disciplined but your "Temple" is a mess, the "Noise" of your actions will drown out the "Truth" of your words.
- **The Father Effect:** Research in the Journal of Marriage and Family shows that "High-Involvement" fathering—specifically when a father provides clear structure and discipline—directly correlates with higher IQ, better emotional regulation, and increased social competence (Lamb, 2010).

Biblical Truth: The Father is the "Chief Systems Officer." He doesn't just provide; he instructs.

"These words, which I am commanding you today, shall be on your heart. You shall teach them diligently to your sons and shall talk of them when you sit in your house and when you walk by the way and when you lie down and when you rise up" (Deuteronomy 6:6-7, NASB). "Train up a child in the way he should go, even when he is old he will not depart from it" (Proverbs 22:6, NASB).

The Site Safety Insight: The Surveillance Camera

Imagine your house has cameras that record everything you do, but the playback is delayed by 20 years. That is parenting.

Your children are 24/7 surveillance cameras. They aren't listening to your lectures; they are recording your habits. If you want them to be kind, you don't give a speech on kindness; you treat the waitress with respect. **You are the message.**

The Solution: The Discipleship Operating System (D.O.S.)

1. **The "Why" Protocol (Lead by Logic):** Just as a good manager explains the "KPIs," a Dominion Father explains the "Why" behind the rule. This shifts the child from "Blind Obedience" (which fails when you aren't looking) to "Internalized Logic." You aren't teaching them to follow orders; you are teaching them to understand the physics of consequence.

2. **The Mirror Habit (Lead by Modeling):** Before you correct a behavior in a child or an employee, audit yourself. Ask: "Am I modeling the 'Scholar' or 'Steward' behavior I am demanding from them?" Leadership is a mirror, not a megaphone. If you want them to read more (Scholar), let them catch you reading. If you want them to be calm (Temple), let them see you regulate your anger.

3. **The Scheduled "Rites of Passage" (Legacy Systems):** Don't leave their growth to chance. Create specific "System

Checks." Every month, take each child (or key team member) out for a "Development Sync." This isn't a lecture; it's a strategy session. Ask: "What is one thing you are struggling to understand right now, and how can I help you build a system to fix it?" This transforms you from a "Boss" into a "Mentor."

INTERACTIVE AUDIT: THE LEGACY LOG

The Premise: You are not just raising children; you are deploying future leaders. Every interaction is a data transfer.

The Trigger: The next time your child (or a team member) fails or disobeys.

The Questions:

1. **The Perspective Shift:** Stop the emotional reaction. Use the Humility System (Chapter 4) to see the failure from their perspective first. [ ] I paused and listened before correcting.

2. **The System Check:** Diagnose the failure. Was it a Scholar issue (they lacked info), a Steward issue (poor resource management), or a Temple issue (lack of self-control)?

3. **The 10-Minute Teach:** Instead of punishing or doing it for them, spend 10 minutes teaching them the System they need to fix it themselves. [ ] I transferred the skill.

The Legacy Oath: "I commit to being the Architect of my home. I will not just manage the madness; I will disciple the future."

Signed: _____

Why This Works

This works because it respects the **Dignity of the Learner**. Whether that learner is 5 years old or a 40-year-old employee, people crave competence. When you stop acting like a "Boss" (barking orders) and start acting like a "Father" (transferring wisdom), you create loyalty. You are giving them the tools to build their own lives, and in doing so, you ensure that your Blueprint survives long after you are gone.

The Next Step

Now that the household is secure, we take these systems into the marketplace. **It is time for Pillar 6: The Entrepreneur (The Instinct of Creation).**

Chapter 6: The Entrepreneur (The Instinct of Creation)

The Master Integrator: Architecting Value Without Sacrificing the Soul

The Pain Point: The Crisis of Misplaced Focus

For years, I misunderstood the role of ambition. I thought having a massive, all-consuming "Goal" was the definition of drive. I didn't realize that a goal, when it becomes your sole focus, ceases to be a target and becomes an Idol.

We are conditioned from birth to **"Work Hard."** It is the mantra of the masculine soul. But rarely does anyone stop to ask: Work hard on what?

Because we lack a clear design, we end up pouring our God-given capacity for labor into the world's default setting: **More**. We grind, we sweat, and we bleed, not building a legacy, but polishing an Idol. We end up working harder on our chains than we do on our freedom.

- **The Distraction:** I worked countless hours with a specific destination in mind—the title, the salary, the status. But the way I perceived that goal acted like a blinder, distracting me from the "Truth" of how things actually work.
- **The False God:** My mind focused on the outcome rather than the System required to sustain it. My first business failed because I was worshiping the "dream" rather than architecting the daily process.
- **The Burnout:** Even when I "succeeded"—climbing into upper management—I was empty. I was burnt out, hated the job, and was missing vital time with my family. I had achieved the goal, but I had destroyed the supporting pillars to get there.

The Crisis: The Personal Script

The Sovereign Intervention It took a career-ending accident to shatter the idol. Stripped of the ability to "grind," I was forced to sit in the silence and re-evaluate the architecture of my life.

I realized that goals aren't inherently evil; they are just diagnostic tools. The error was in making the goal the **Master** rather than the **Servant**. In my recovery, I began to work on **Systems** to operate my life. I prioritized my time, managed my family interactions with intention, and audited my spiritual health. The result? I didn't just recover; I was brought closer to **GOD.** I learned that when you focus on the "System" (His way of operating), the right goals are achieved as a natural byproduct, without the sacrifice of your peace or your purpose.

The Core Concept: The Genetic Code of the Creator

To understand this pillar, we must look deeper than "business." Why do you feel a burning desire to build, fix, and scale things? It is not just capitalism; it is **Creation.**

You are created in the Imago Dei—the Image of God. The Bible opens with the ultimate act of entrepreneurship: God takes a "market" that is void and without form (Chaos) and implements a system of light, land, and life (Order) to create value.

- **The Inheritance:** You have inherited this "creative genetics." When you organize a team, launch a product, or

even fix a broken routine in your home, you are mirroring the Creator's nature to bring order out of chaos.
- **The Shift:** We do not build to serve the Idol of Money; we build to exercise the Instinct of the Architect. When you build for money, you are a slave to the market. When you build to exercise your design, money ceases to be the Master and becomes the Fuel

The Application: Beyond the Boardroom A Dominion Man realizes that "Entrepreneurship" is not a job title; it is a way of **interacting with reality**. It is the refusal to accept chaos in any domain.

- **For the Business Owner**: You are building systems to serve customers and employees. You create value where there was none.
- **For the Employee (The Intrapreneur):** You don't need an LLC to be an Entrepreneur. If you take a chaotic process at your job and streamline it, you are exercising Dominion. You are bringing Order to your corner of the Creation.
- **For the Family Man (The Home Builder):** Your household is the most important startup you will ever launch. It has culture, logistics, and resource management. When you design a system for chores, or architect a weekly family meeting to reduce chaos, you are not just "parenting"; you are exercising the Instinct of Creation to build a dynasty.

The Site Insight: The General Contractor

The "Self-Made Man" is a myth. A Master Electrician can wire a house, but he can't build one alone. He needs the Plumber, the Framer, and the Roofer.

The Entrepreneur is simply the **General Contractor**. He holds the blueprints (The Vision), but he knows he cannot lay every brick. If you try to be the Architect, the Builder, and the Laborer, the project fails. Dominion is recognizing that you need a **Brotherhood** of specialists to finish the job.

The Evidence: Systems Over Idols

Scholarly Evidence:

- **The Progress Principle:** Research by Amabile and Kramer (2011) demonstrates that "small wins"—making progress in a meaningful system—is the single most powerful driver of motivation, far exceeding the "big win" of the final goal. Focusing on the system creates a "progress loop" that prevents burnout.
- **The 94/6 Rule:** Quality expert W. Edwards Deming famously stated that 94% of failures are caused by the system, not the person. If you are struggling in your marriage or business, don't just "try harder" (Goal); fix the architecture (System).
- **Work Orientation Theory:** Research distinguishes between a "Job" (financial focus), a "Career" (status focus),

and a "Calling" (fulfillment focus). The Dominion Entrepreneur operates in the "Calling" orientation, viewing their systems as a contribution to the greater good, which paradoxically leads to higher financial performance (Wrzesniewski et al., 1997).

Biblical Truth: The Bible consistently points us away from the "Idol of the Result" and toward the "Wisdom of the Build."

"What profit is there to the graven image... for the maker of his fortune trusts in his own handiwork?" (Habakkuk 2:18, NASB). "By wisdom a house is built, and by understanding it is established; and by knowledge the rooms are filled with all precious and pleasant riches" (Proverbs 24:3-4, NASB). Note the order: Wisdom (The Blueprint) comes before the Riches (The Goal).

The Foreman's Insight: Hitting Singles

Everyone wants to hit the Grand Slam (The Million Dollar Exit). But if you swing for the fences every time, you strike out. The Hall of Fame is filled with guys who just hit singles.

"Small Wins" are singles. You hit a single in your sales process. You hit a single in your family dinner schedule. Enough singles load the bases. Then, the Grand Slam happens by accident. Stop swinging for the fences; start hitting the ball.

The Solution: The Industry Operating System (I.O.S.)

1. **The Idol Audit (Scholar System):** Ask: "Is my current goal a result of a system I'm building, or a destination I'm chasing at the expense of my other pillars?" If the pursuit of the goal is destroying the Temple (Health) or the Covenant (Marriage), it is an Idol.

2. **The Universal Value Protocol:** Apply "Customer Discovery" to your inner circle. Stop guessing what your wife or children need. Interview them. Collect data. Build a system to deliver that value consistently.

3. **The Sabbath Protocol (Temple System):** A true Architect can walk away from the building because the structure is sound. If your industry or home requires your 24/7 presence, your architecture is failing. The Sabbath is the ultimate proof that you trust the Creator more than your own grind.

INTERACTIVE AUDIT: THE CREATION LOG

The Premise: Are you a slave to the "Goal," or a Master of the "System"?

The Trigger: Next time you feel "burnt out" or overwhelmed by a massive, distant goal.

The Questions:

1. The Idol Check: Step away for 30 minutes. Look at your blueprints. Is your current "Grind" destroying your Temple or your Covenant? [ ] Yes [ ] No

2. The System Check: Identify the System Failure. What is the one small thing broken in your process that is causing the friction? (e.g., lack of delegation, unclear communication).

3. The Single: Don't set a goal to "make a million dollars." Set a System Goal for today (e.g., "Document the sales script"). Write it below.

The Creation Oath: "I refuse to worship the outcome. I commit to building the System, honoring the Sabbath, and trusting the Creator with the results."

Signed:

_____

Why This Works

This works because it aligns your **Ambition** with **Reality**. Ambition without a system is just anxiety. By shifting your focus from the "Goal" (which you cannot control) to the "System" (which you can control), you regain agency. You stop living in the future—where anxiety lives—and start building in the present—where Dominion happens.

The Next Step

When you master the Instinct of Creation, you stop working for a living and start designing a life. But to keep that design from collapsing under its own weight, you need the final piece of the puzzle: The Man who holds it all together.

It is time to conclude our initial training with Chapter 7: The Man (The System of Systems).

Chapter 7: The Man (The System of Systems)

The General Contractor: Excavating the Image of God

The Pain Point: The Exhaustion of the Chameleon

You have made it this far. You have analyzed the components of your mind (Scholar), your money (Steward), your body (Temple), and your relationships (Husband/Father/Entrepreneur). You have the blueprints in your hand.

But blueprints are heavy.

If we are honest, right now, you might not feel like a **Master Builder**. You might feel like a tired juggler standing in the middle of a construction site that is half-finished. You are terrified that if you drop one ball—if you miss one mortgage payment, one date night, or one workout—the whole structure will collapse.

You are exhausted because you are suffering from **The Chameleon Effect.**

- **At Work:** You put on the mask of **The Machine, The Closer, The Boss**. You project invincibility because weakness is a liability.
- **At Home:** You put on the mask of the **Patient Dad** and the **Loving Husband**. You suppress your stress to keep the peace.
- **In the Circle:** You put on the mask of the **Reliable Friend** or the **Wise Mentor**. You carry everyone else's burdens while secretly crushing under your own.
- **At Church:** You put on the mask of the **Holy Man**. You sit in the pew and nod, terrified that someone might see the cracks in your armor.

You are constantly switching masks to fit the "Role" required of you. Psychological research refers to this as **"Compartmentalization."** While it feels like a safety mechanism to keep your work stress away from your family, studies show that maintaining these separate "selves" inevitably leads to emotional fragility and lower self-esteem.

Deep down, in the quiet moments when the house is asleep, you ask the question every man asks but rarely admits: "If I stopped performing... would I still exist? Would everything function without me?"

The Crisis: Instrumental vs. Intrinsic Value The world judges a man by his **Instrumental Value**—what he can be used for. A hammer has value only as long as it drives nails. If the hammer breaks, you throw it away. Many of us feel like tools. We feel valuable only when we are providing, protecting, or producing.

But this is a lie that leads to the grave. If your worth is tied to your output, then your identity is always one bad quarter, one layoff, or one divorce away from annihilation.

The Personal Script: The Man in the Mirror I lived as a "Human Doing" for decades. I avoided the mirror because I didn't like the man staring back. I saw a fraud. I saw a man who was great at building businesses but terrible at being at peace.

When my accident stripped away my ability to "do"—when I couldn't work, couldn't lift, couldn't perform—I was left with nothing but the reflection. I had to answer the terrifying question: **"Who is Paul Stone if Paul Stone isn't building anything?"**

I wish I could tell you that I found the answer instantly. I didn't.

In that silence, I didn't discover the System—I only discovered the structural failure. I was still lost. I was still mentally worshipping the

"Goal" (the comeback, the next deal, the recovery), but my body and soul were on strike. Out of sheer necessity, I began to shore up the foundations just to survive. I started prioritizing my health because I was broken. I started listening to my wife because I was lonely.

I didn't know I was building a "Dominion Design" at the time. I was just trying to stop the bleeding. But looking back, that was the excavation phase. I had to hit bedrock before I could pour the concrete for what you are reading today.

The Two Tiers of Manhood

To understand "The Man," you must understand the architecture of your own soul. The six pillars are divided into two specific categories: **The Non-Negotiables** (The Foundation) and **The Instincts** (The Expression).

Tier 1: The Non-Negotiables (The Foundation)

- **The Pillars:** Scholar, Steward, Temple.
- **The Nature:** Taught Discipline.
- **The Function:** Self-Governance.

These are not instincts. You were not born with a balanced budget, a disciplined mind, or a strong body. These are **Disciplines** that must be taught, learned, and maintained.

- **The Scholar:** We must learn to filter truth (Proverbs 4:7).

- **The Steward:** We must learn to manage resources (Matthew 25:14-30).
- **The Temple:** We must discipline the body (1 Corinthians 9:27).

Scholarly Evidence: Aristotle, the father of virtue ethics, argued that human flourishing (Eudaimonia) is not a feeling, but an activity of the soul in accordance with virtue. He taught that character is not innate; it is formed by Habituation—doing the right thing over and over until it becomes second nature. Without these foundational habits, the man collapses under the weight of his own life.

Tier 2: The Instincts (The Expression)

- **The Pillars:** Husband, Father, Entrepreneur.
- **The Nature:** Created Essence.
- **The Function:** Dominion.

These are instincts. You do not need to be taught to want a mate (Husband). You do not need to be taught to protect your lineage (Father). You do not need to be taught to create and build (Entrepreneur). These desires are burned into your genetic code.

Biblical Truth: The Imago Dei This is the **Image of God** (Imago Dei). "God created man in His own image, in the image of God He created him" (Genesis 1:27). Biblical scholars note that in the

Ancient Near East, an "image" was not just a picture; it was a functional representative. An image carried the essence and authority of the king into the territory.

- **Husband:** Mirrors God's Covenant nature.
- **Father:** Mirrors God's Paternal nature.
- **Entrepreneur:** Mirrors God's Creative nature.

The Cycle of Dominion

Here is the secret sauce. Here is why most men fail. **You cannot sustain the Instincts (Tier 2) without the Non-Negotiables (Tier 1).**

- **The Breakdown:** You have the instinct to be a great **Father**, but if you lack the **Scholar** (Wisdom) and the **Temple** (Patience/Energy), you will yell at your kids instead of discipling them.
- **The Breakdown:** You have the instinct to be a great Entrepreneur, but if you lack the Steward (Financial Discipline), you will bankrupt the company chasing a dream.
- **The Breakdown:** You have the instinct to be a loyal Lead Partner (Husband, Friend, or Boss), but if you lack the Scholar (Humility to hear truth) and the Temple (Emotional Regulation), you will burn bridges the moment pressure mounts—turning allies into enemies whether in the bedroom or the boardroom.

The Cycle works like this:

- **The Creator** installs the Instincts (Desire).
- **The Man** builds the Non-Negotiables (Discipline).
- **The Discipline** fuels the Instincts to produce Dominion.

The Prototype: The Whole Man

If you want to know what this looks like in practice, look at the only man who ever did it perfectly. Jesus was not just a "spiritual teacher." He was the **System of Systems** in flesh.

- The Scholar: At age 12, He was in the temple, listening and asking questions (Luke 2:46). He mastered the texts.
- **The Steward:** He managed resources miraculously (feeding the 5,000) but lived simply, ensuring nothing was wasted (John 6:12).
- **The Temple:** He frequently withdrew to the wilderness to sleep and pray, regulating His energy before pouring it out (Luke 5:16).

Because He mastered the Non-Negotiables, He perfectly executed the Instincts:

- **The Husband:** He laid down His life for His Bride (The Church).
- **The Father:** He discipled the Twelve, calling them "Little Children" (John 13:33).

- **The Entrepreneur:** He built a Kingdom that has outlasted every empire in history.

Biblical Truth: "He is the image of the invisible God, the firstborn of all creation" (Colossians 1:15). Jesus came to remind us of who we are. He didn't come to make us "religious"; He came to restore the **Imago Dei**—to show us how to be Human again.

The Solution: Identity Integration

So, how do you fix the fragmentation? How do you stop being a Chameleon? You must move from Performance-Based **Identity to Integrated Identity.**

Scholarly Evidence: Research on "Identity Integration" shows that when a person's external roles (Work, Family) align with their internal values (Faith/Identity), their psychological stress drops, and their resilience skyrockets. Psychologist William **Swann's Self-Verification Theory** proves that we are desperate for coherence. We need our "outside" to match our "inside".

The Keystone Concept: The Architecture of Wholeness Most men are not looking for more "hacks"; they are looking for Wholeness. You feel scattered because you are trying to build a life around a center that cannot hold the weight of your soul.

In architecture, the **Keystone** is the central wedge at the summit of an arch. It locks all other stones into place. If the Keystone is the wrong shape or size, the arch doesn't just look bad; it collapses.

- **The Impostor:** If your Keystone is "Money," the weight of the Steward pillar crushes the Father pillar. You provide for your kids, but you are never with them.
- **The Impostor:** If your Keystone is "Success," the Entrepreneur pillar crushes the Temple pillar. You build a great company, but your body rots from the inside out.
- **The Truth:** The only Keystone that creates structural integrity is the one found in the Creator's Manual: The Truth of Sonship.

When you accept the Truth—that you are a Son of the Architect and not a slave to the Market—the arch locks into place.

- You don't have to perform to be valuable; you perform because you are valuable.
- You don't have to earn rest; you rest because it is your inheritance.

This is the key to completeness. You are not the sum of your pillars. You are the General Contractor who manages them, standing securely under the Keystone of the Truth.

The Site Superintendent's Insight: The General Contractor

A Subcontractor panics when it rains. A General Contractor (GC) knows rain is part of the schedule. The GC doesn't try to hold up the walls with his bare hands. He relies on the Foundation (Christ) and the Framing (The Systems).

- When your finances get tight, the "Fragmented Man" panics. The "GC" looks at the Steward Protocol and adjusts the budget.
- When your marriage gets rocky, the "Fragmented Man" runs away. The "GC" looks at the Covenant Protocol and initiates a repair.

You are not the building. You are the Manager of the Building.

INTERACTIVE AUDIT: THE MIRROR LOG

The Premise: The man you want to be—the calm, strong, integrated man—is not a stranger you need to find. He is buried under the noise.

The Trigger: Go to the bathroom. Lock the door. Turn on the light. Look in the mirror.

The Questions:

1. The Confession: Say this out loud: "I am tired of performing. I am tired of the masks. I am done being a Chameleon." [ ] I said it.

2. The Truth: Say this out loud: "I am not what I produce. I am not my bank account. I am a Son of the Architect. I have the Instincts of the Creator in my blood." [ ] I said it.

3. The Commission: Say this out loud: "I will build the Non-Negotiables (Scholar, Steward, Temple) so that I can release the Instincts (Husband, Father, Entrepreneur)." [ ] I said it.

The Identity Oath: "I refuse to be a Fragmented Man. I commit to integrating my life under the Dominion of the Architect."

Signed:

_____

Why This Works

This works because it stops the **Identity War**. Most men are exhausted because they are fighting a civil war inside their own chests—"Who I am" vs. "What I do."

When you integrate the system, the war ends. You stop performing for approval and start operating from approval. You realize that Dominion is not about conquering the world; it is about conquering the chaos within yourself so that you can bless the world.

The Bridge: Why You Must Enter The Lab

You now have the knowledge. But "knowledge puffs up, but love builds up" (1 Corinthians 8:1, NASB). Reading a book about pushups doesn't build muscle. Reading a book about Dominion doesn't build a life.

You are standing at the edge of the job site. The blueprints are rolled out. The crew is waiting. It is time to put down the book and pick up the shovel.

I cannot build your house for you. But I can walk with you onto the site. Welcome to the construction phase.

Welcome to The Dominion Lab.

Conclusion: The Groundbreaking

From Blueprint to Broken Ground

We have reached the end of the pages, but we are only at the beginning of the work.

Over the last seven chapters, we have dismantled the chaos. We have excavated the debris of the "Friendly Ghost" and the "Passenger." We have looked at the **Scholar**, the **Steward**, and the **Temple**—not as burdens to carry, but as the Non-Negotiables required to keep you alive. We have uncovered the **Husband,** the **Father,** and the **Entrepreneur**—not as roles you play, but as Instincts given to you by the Creator to establish Dominion.

We have drawn the connection between the discipline of the Foundation and the freedom of Expression. We have seen the **Whole Man**—the **Integrated Builder** who stops juggling masks and starts building a legacy.

The Friction of the Start I know the friction you are feeling right now. I know it because I feel it every morning. It is the friction between Knowing and Doing.

There is a part of you—the old, fragmented Chameleon—that wants to close this book, nod your head, and go back to the way things were. It wants to go back to the "comfortable drowning" because the work of excavation seems too hard. That voice is lying to you. It is telling you that you are alone in this.

You are not alone.

I am not writing this from a finished palace; I am writing this from the job site. I am still checking my mirrors. I am still auditing my stewardship. I am still repenting to my wife when I miss the mark. We are on this ride together. The only difference is that now, we have a map.

The General Contractor's Charge You are no longer a Passenger in a Bulldozer. You are the General Contractor of your life.

- When the rain comes (and it will), you will not panic; you will check the roof.
- When the noise returns (and it will), you will not listen; you will check the Keystone.

You have the blueprints. You have the tools. You have the permission of the King to take back your territory. Do not let this moment pass. Do not let the "noise" rush back in and steal this clarity.

The world does not need another busy man. It does not need another rich man. It does not need another tired man. The world needs You. The real You. The Integrated You. The Man who reflects the Architect.

We are building a Brotherhood of men who have decided to stop apologizing for their strength and start sanctifying it. We are waiting for you in the Lab.

Put down the book. Pick up the shovel. **Let's get to work.** This is only the ground floor. We have secured the perimeter. In the coming months, we will be releasing deep-dive blueprints for every pillar established here. Stay vigilant. The build continues.

— **Paul Stone**

ACKNOWLEDGMENTS

No man builds alone.

While my name is on the cover, this structure was raised by a crew of men and women who held the ladder, checked the plumb lines, and refused to let me quit.

To the Brotherhood who tested these systems in the mud of real life—thank you for your honesty.

To the mentors who handed me their own battered blueprints when I was drowning in noise—thank you for the light.

And to the King—for giving a broken man a shovel and a second chance.

Connect with the Brotherhood

This journey is not meant to be walked in isolation. You are now a recruit of the M.M.E.T. (Modern Men Excavation Team)—the brotherhood that builds the Dominion Systems.

- **The M.M.E.T. Line:** Text "DIG" to (804) 214-6638

- **The Dominion Lab:** www.thedominionlab.com

- **Facebook:** @PaulStoneDominion

- **Instagram:** @paulstonedominion.com

- **TikTok:** @paulstonedominion

THE DOMINION KEYS

A Chapter-by-Chapter Reference Guide

Introduction: The Site Survey

The Conceptual Keys

- **The Passenger:** The passive state of moving through life without control.
- **The Bulldozer:** The destructive force of uncontrolled success or busyness.
- **The Architect:** The persona of intentional design and self-governance.
- **Dominion:** The biblical mandate to create order from chaos.
- **The Hypocrisy:** The realization that we build systems for work but not for life.

The Scriptural Keys

- **Proverbs 22:6** — "Train up a child in the way he should go..."
- **Proverbs 22:13** — "The sluggard says, 'There is a lion outside...'"
- **Psalm 127:1** — "Unless the Lord builds the house, they labor in vain who build it."
- **1 Corinthians 3:10** — "...like a wise master builder I laid a foundation."
- **Genesis 1:28** — "Be fruitful and multiply... and subdue it."

- **Matthew 23:28** — "...on the inside you are full of hypocrisy and lawlessness."

Chapter 1: The Scholar

The Conceptual Keys

- **Filtration:** The active process of blocking "Noise" to protect "Truth."
- **Anchor Bias:** The tendency to rely on the first piece of information received.
- **Imposter Participants:** External voices that hijack decision-making.
- **The Fear of the Lord:** The ultimate filter for data.
- **Input Analysis:** The audit of what you allow into your mind.

The Scriptural Keys

- **1 John 2:7** — "...an old commandment which you have had from the beginning."
- **Proverbs 9:10** — "The fear of the Lord is the beginning of wisdom."
- **Proverbs 4:23** — "Watch over your heart with all diligence..."
- **Psalm 1:1** — "How blessed is the man who does not walk in the counsel of the wicked."
- **Psalm 5:3** — "In the morning, O Lord, You will hear my voice..."

- **1 John 4:1** — "...test the spirits to see whether they are from God."
- **Romans 12:2** — "Be transformed by the renewing of your mind."

Chapter 2: The Steward

The Conceptual Keys

- **Fiduciary:** Managing resources for the benefit of God and Legacy.
- **The 80/10/10 Protocol:** The mathematical constraint for financial discipline. (Live on 80%, Save 10%, Give 10%).
- **Entropy:** The natural tendency of unmanaged systems to decline.
- **Scarcity Mindset:** The trap that reduces bandwidth and fuels anxiety.
- **Sabbath:** The constraint that proves trust in the Provider.

The Scriptural Keys

- **1 Corinthians 4:2** — "It is required of stewards that one be found trustworthy."
- **Proverbs 3:9** — "Honor the Lord from your wealth..."
- **Romans 8:20-21** — "For the creation was subjected to futility..."
- **Matthew 25:25** — "I was afraid, and went away and hid your talent..."
- **Mark 2:27** — "The Sabbath was made for man, and not man for the Sabbath."

Chapter 3: The Temple

The Conceptual Keys

- **Structural Integrity:** Health as utility (load-bearing capacity).
- **BDNF:** The biological link between movement and wisdom.
- **Maintenance Debt:** The accumulated cost of neglecting the machine.
- **The Spotter:** The necessity of brotherhood for heavy lifting.
- **The 168 Protocol:** Managing the hours of the week for recovery and load.

The Scriptural Keys

- **2 Timothy 2:21** — "...he will be a vessel for honor, sanctified, useful to the Master..."
- **1 Corinthians 9:27** — "I discipline my body and make it my slave..."
- **Galatians 6:7** — "...whatever a man sows, this he will also reap."
- **Ecclesiastes 4:9-10** — "Two are better than one... for if either of them falls..."
- **Ephesians 5:16** — "Making the most of your time, because the days are evil."
- **1 Corinthians 6:19-20** — "Your body is a temple of the Holy Spirit..."

Chapter 4: The Husband

The Conceptual Keys

- **Covenant vs. Contract:** Unconditional faithfulness vs. transactional liability.
- **Cognitive Empathy:** Understanding the partner's data before reacting.
- **The Lead Partner:** Assuming liability for the emotional culture.
- **The Relief Valve:** Using Brotherhood to vent pressure safely.
- **The 5:1 Ratio:** The balance of positive to negative interactions.

The Scriptural Keys

- **Jeremiah 31:33** — "I will be their God, and they shall be My people."
- **1 Peter 3:7** — "Husbands, live with your wives in an understanding way..."
- **Ephesians 5:23** — "For the husband is the head of the wife, as Christ also is the head of the church..."
- **James 5:16** — "Confess your sins to one another... so that you may be healed."
- **Ephesians 4:29** — "Let no unwholesome word proceed from your mouth..."

Chapter 5: The Father

The Conceptual Keys

- **Social Learning:** Learning by observation (modeling).
- **The Friendly Ghost:** The failure of absenteeism or permissiveness.
- **Discipleship:** Transferring the "Source Code" to the next generation.
- **The Father Effect:** The impact of paternal presence on competence.
- **Incarnational Principle:** Being the message rather than just speaking it.

The Scriptural Keys

- **John 13:15** — "For I gave you an example that you also should do as I did to you."
- **Proverbs 13:24** — "He who spares his rod hates his son..."
- **1 Timothy 5:8** — "But if anyone does not provide for his own..."
- **Matthew 28:19** — "Make disciples of all the nations..."
- **Proverbs 17:6** — "The glory of sons is their fathers."
- **Deuteronomy 6:6-7** — "You shall teach them diligently to your sons..."

Chapter 6: The Entrepreneur

The Conceptual Keys

- **Imago Dei:** The "Image of God" as the source of the creative instinct.
- **The Progress Principle:** Motivation driven by "small wins."
- Idol Audit: Identifying false gods in your goals.
- **General Contractor:** Managing the system rather than doing all the labor.
- **Work Orientation:** Moving from Job to Calling

The Scriptural Keys

- **Genesis 1:27** — "God created man in His own image..."
- **Luke 16:10** — "He who is faithful in a very little thing is faithful also **in much."**
- **1 John 5:21** — "Little children, guard yourselves from idols."
- **1 Corinthians 12:21** — "The eye cannot say to the hand, 'I have no need of you'..."
- **Colossians 3:23** — "Do your work heartily, as for the Lord..."
- **Habakkuk 2:18** — "What profit is there to the graven image...?"

Chapter 7: The Man

The Conceptual Keys

- **The Chameleon Effect:** The exhaustion of wearing different masks.
- **Identity Integration:** Aligning external roles with internal values.
- **Habituation:** Character formed by doing.
- **The Keystone**: Identity in Sonship holding the arch together.
- **Instrumental Value:** The lie that value equals output.

The Scriptural Keys

- **James 1:8** — "A double-minded man is unstable in all his ways."
- **Psalm 86:11** — "Unite my heart to fear Your name."
- **1 Timothy 4:7** — "Discipline yourself for the purpose of godliness."
- **Ephesians 2:20** — "Christ Jesus Himself being the corner stone..."
- **1 John 3:1** — "See how great a love the Father has bestowed on us..."

Conclusion: The Commission

The Conceptual Keys

- **The Groundbreaking:** The transition from theory to action.
- **The Friction:** The resistance between Knowing and Doing.
- **The Commission:** The authorization to take dominion.

The Scriptural Keys

- **James 1:22** — "But prove yourselves doers of the word, and not merely hearers..."
- **Luke 13:24** — "Strive to enter through the narrow door..."

References

Amabile, T. M., & Kramer, S. J. (2011). *The progress principle: Using small wins to ignite joy, engagement, and creativity at work.* Harvard Business Review Press.

Aristotle. (2000). *Nicomachean ethics* (R. Crisp, Trans.). Cambridge University Press.

Bandura, A. (1977). *Social learning theory.* Prentice-Hall.

Brickman, P., & Campbell, D. T. (1971). Hedonic relativism and planning the good society. In M. H. Appley (Ed.), *Adaptation-level theory* (pp. 287–305). Academic Press.

Çengel, Y. A., & Boles, M. A. (2015). *Thermodynamics: An engineering approach* (8th ed.). McGraw-Hill Education.

Deming, W. E. (1982). *Out of the crisis.* MIT Press.

Erickson, K. I., Voss, M. W., Prakash, R. S., Basak, C., Szabo, A., Chaddock, L., ... & Kramer, A. F. (2011). Exercise training increases size of hippocampus and improves memory. *Proceedings of the National Academy of Sciences, 108*(7), 3017–3022.

Gottman, J. M. (1994). *Why marriages succeed or fail: And how you can make yours last.* Simon & Schuster.

Huston, D. (2010). *Structural sensing, health monitoring, and performance evaluation.* CRC Press.

Lamb, M. E. (2010). *The role of the father in child development* (5th ed.). Wiley.

Legal Information Institute. (2023). Fiduciary duty. Cornell Law School. https://www.law.cornell.edu/wex/fiduciary_duty

Lidwell, W., Holden, K., & Butler, J. (2010). *Universal principles of design*. Rockport Publishers.

Markman, H. J., Stanley, S. M., & Blumberg, S. L. (2010). *Fighting for your marriage*. Jossey-Bass.

Mullainathan, S., & Shafir, E. (2013). *Scarcity: Why having so little means so much*. Times Books.

New American Standard Bible. (2020). Zondervan. (Original work published 1960).

Parkinson, C. N. (1955). Parkinson's Law. *The Economist*.

Rebar, A. L., Stanton, R., Geard, D., Short, C., Duncan, M. J., & Vandelanotte, C. (2015). A meta-meta-analysis of the effect of physical activity on depression and anxiety in non-clinical adult populations. *Health Psychology Review, 9*(3), 366–378.

Ryan, R. M., & Deci, E. L. (2000). Self-determination theory and the facilitation of intrinsic motivation, social development, and well-being. *American Psychologist, 55*(1), 68–78.

Schwardmann, P., Tripodi, E., & van der Weele, J. J. (2022). Self-persuasion: Evidence from relevant experts. *The Review of Economic Studies, 89*(4), 2203–2235.

Showers, C. J., & Zeigler-Hill, V. (2007). Compartmentalization and integration: The role of self-structure in emotional well-being. In C. Sedikides & S. J. Spencer (Eds.), The self (pp. 217–232). Psychology Press.

Stokes, P. D. (2005). *Creativity from constraints: The psychology of breakthrough.* Springer Publishing Company.

Swann, W. B. (2011). Self-verification theory. In P. A. M. Van Lange, A. W. Kruglanski, & E. T. Higgins (Eds.), Handbook of theories of social psychology (Vol. 2, pp. 23–42). Sage Publications.

Talbert, B. M. (2017). Overthinking and other minds: The analysis paralysis. *Social Epistemology, 31*(6), 545–556.

The Decision Lab. (2024). Anchoring bias. https://thedecisionlab.com/biases/anchoring-bias

Walker, M. (2017). *Why we sleep: Unlocking the power of sleep and dreams.* Scribner.

Walton, J. H. (2001). *Genesis.* Zondervan.

Wrzesniewski, A., McCauley, C., Rozin, P., & Schwartz, B. (1997). Jobs, careers, and callings: People's relations to their work. Journal of Research in Personality, 31(1), 21–33.

ABOUT THE AUTHOR

Paul Stone is not a guru. He is a builder.

After spending years chasing the world's definition of success—and nearly losing his family and his peace in the process—Paul realized that modern men are drowning because they are trying to drive a bulldozer without a manual.

He founded The Dominion Lab to excavate the ancient blueprints of the Imago Dei (Image of God) and operationalize them for the modern world.

But this is not a solo project. Paul is driven by a deep excitement to serve the Brotherhood. He views this mission not as a podium to teach from, but as a job site to grow on. He is committed to sharpening his own iron alongside every man who picks up a shovel.

Paul lives with his wife and children, where he is still learning to master the art of being a General Contractor for his home.

He is currently working on the next phase of the build.

www.ingramcontent.com/pod-product-compliance
Lightning Source LLC
Chambersburg PA
CBHW060502110426
42738CB00055B/2553